Ecosystems
Boreal Forests

Patricia Miller-Schroeder

www.av2books.com

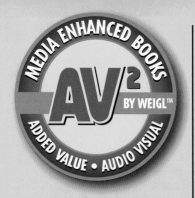

AV² provides enriched content that supplements and complements this book Weigl's AV² books strive to create inspired learning and engage young minds in a total learning experience.

Your AV² Media Enhanced books come alive with...

Audio
Listen to sections of the book read aloud.

Key Words
Study vocabulary, and complete a matching word activity.

Video
Watch informative video clips.

Quizzes
Test your knowledge.

Embedded Weblinks
Gain additional information for research.

Slide Show
View images and captions, and prepare a presentation.

Try This!
Complete activities and hands-on experiments.

... and much, much more

Go to **www.av2books.com**, and enter this book's unique code.

BOOK CODE

B 6 6 2 6 1 7

AV² by Weigl brings you media enhanced books that support active learning.

Published by AV² by Weigl
350 5th Avenue, 59th Floor
New York, NY 10118
Website: www.av2books.com   www.weigl.com

Library of Congress Cataloging-in-Publication Data

Miller-Schroeder, Patricia.
 Boreal forests / Patricia Miller-Schroeder.
   p. cm. -- (Ecosystems)
 Includes index.
 ISBN 978-1-61690-642-9 (hardcover : alk. paper) -- ISBN 978-1-61690-648-1 (softcover : alk. paper)
 1. Taiga ecology--Juvenile literature. I. Title.
 QH541.5.T3M55 2011
 577.3'7--dc22

                              2010050984

Printed in the United States of America in North Mankato, Minnesota
1 2 3 4 5 6 7 8 9 0 15 14 13 12 11

052011
WEP37500

Project Coordinator Aaron Carr
Design Sonja Vogel

Every reasonable effort has been made to trace ownership and to obtain permission to reprint copyright material. The publishers would be pleased to have any errors or omissions brought to their attention so that they may be corrected in subsequent printings.

Photo Credits
Weigl acknowledges Getty Images as its primary photo supplier for this title.

Contents

What is a Boreal Forest Ecosystem?

Boreal forest rivers are fed by mountain glaciers. Animals can use rivers in the boreal forest for travel, food, and as a source of water.

Earth is home to millions of different **organisms**, all of which have specific survival needs. These organisms rely on their environment, or the place where they live, for their survival. All plants and animals have relationships with their environment. They interact with the environment itself, as well as the other plants and animals within the environment. These interactions create an **ecosystem**.

The boreal forest is the largest ecosystem on Earth. It stretches 50 million acres (20 million hectares) in a band across North America, Europe, and Asia. Cold north winds blow across the snow-covered land for much of the year. During the brief summer months, fires sometimes flare, destroying parts of the forest.

The boreal forest is home to many organisms that have adapted to this environment. Animals such as timber wolves, grizzly bears, lynx, moose, caribou, beavers, and voles live here. **Migratory** birds from warblers to whooping cranes spend their summers in the forest. Colorful mushrooms and **lichens** grow under the tall evergreen trees.

Eco Facts

Mushrooms play a key role in the boreal forest. Some mushrooms act as recyclers by breaking down dead plant and animal matter. Others provide nutrition for trees. Many animals in the forest use mushrooms as a food source.

Within the boreal forest are two main types of forests. One is called a "closed forest" because the trees grow close together. These forests are shady, and the forest floor is covered with velvety moss. The second type of boreal forest is called lichen woodland. The trees here are farther apart, leaving more open areas where lichens grow.

Levels of Organization in Boreal Forest Ecosystems

Ecosystems can be broken down into levels of organization. These levels range from a single plant or animal to many **species** of plants and animals living together in an area.

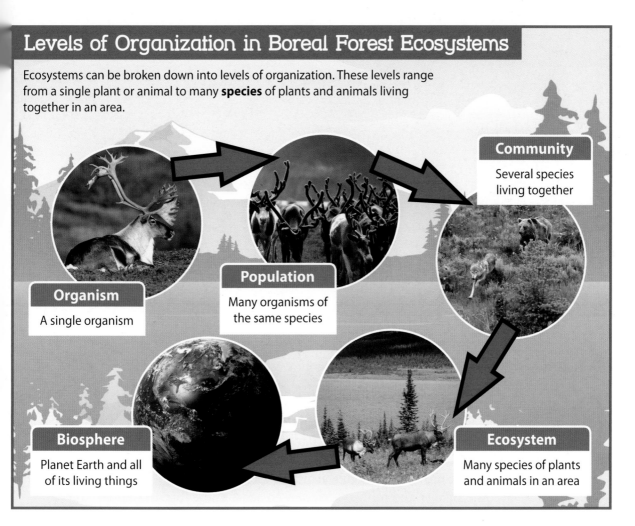

Organism
A single organism

Population
Many organisms of the same species

Community
Several species living together

Ecosystem
Many species of plants and animals in an area

Biosphere
Planet Earth and all of its living things

Where in the World?

North America's boreal forest stretches more than 6,214 miles (10,000 kilometers) across the continent.

The boreal forest stretches across the northern parts of North America, Europe, and Asia, forming a circle. The forest's northern boundaries meet the treeless arctic plains, or tundra. This border parallels an imaginary line called an **isotherm**. Here, the average July temperature is about 50° Fahrenheit (10° Celsius). This temperature provides enough warmth in the summer for the trees to grow. The trees become smaller and more widely spaced apart as the forest extends farther north.

Deciduous forests and grasslands grow on the southern border of the boreal forest. This boundary parallels an isotherm where the average July temperature does not rise above 65° F (18° C). The evergreen trees of the boreal forest blend with the deciduous trees of the more southern forests.

The North American boreal forest stretches across the continent from Labrador in the east to Alaska in the west. In some areas, this boreal forest extends more than 1,250 miles (2,000 km) from north to south. Canada contains 25 percent of Earth's boreal forest.

The European and Asian boreal forest stretches from Siberia in the east to Scandinavia in the west. In Asia, the boreal forest is 1,850 miles (3,000 km) from north to south at its widest point. More than 50 percent of Earth's boreal forests are in Russia. Norway, Sweden, and Finland together have 4 percent of Earth's total boreal forest, while Mongolia and China have 3 percent.

Eco Facts

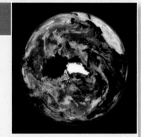

Together, the boreal forests of North America, Europe, and Asia cover 4.6 million square miles (12 million sq. km). This is larger than the total size of either the United States or Canada.

During the Ice Age about 18,000 years ago, much of the area that is now boreal forest was covered by glaciers up to 1 mile (1.6 km) thick.

Boreal forest snow is often soft and fluffy when it falls. A pail full of taiga snow will melt down to only 1 inch (2.5 centimeters) of water in the bottom of the pail.

Boreal forests are sometimes called taiga, northern forests, snow forests, or **coniferous** forests. *Taiga* is a Russian word that means "marshy pine forest."

Boreal forests contain bogs, fens, marshes, and lakes, as well as trees.

Mapping the Boreal Forests

Boreal Forest ecosystems are found in the Northern Hemisphere. This map shows where the world's major boreal forests are located. Find the place where you live on the map. Which boreal forest is closest to where you live?

Legend

■ Boreal Forests

□ Ocean

∿ River

Scale at Equator

```
0      1,000    2,000    3,000 miles
|        |        |        |
0    1,000    2,000    3,000 km
```

N

Wrangell–St. Elias National Park, United States

Newfoundland Highland Fores Canada

ARCTIC OCEAN

Alaskan Peninsula Montane Taiga, United States

Canadian Shield Boreal Forest, Canada

NORTH PACIFIC OCEAN

NORTH AMERICA

NORTH ATLANTIC OCEAN

EQUATOR

SOUTH AMERICA

SOUTH PACIFIC OCEAN

Tongass National Forest

Location: Alaska, United States
Size: 26,250 square miles (67,990 sq. km)
Fact: The Tongass is the largest national forest in the United States. It is home to a diverse variety of plant and animal life. This forest is home to 500-year-old trees, about 1,700 coastal grizzly bears, and the largest concentration of bald eagles found anywhere in the world.

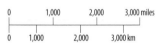

Northern Ontario Boreal Forest

Location: Ontario, Canada
Size: 178,300 square miles (461,700 sq. km)
Fact: The Northern Ontario Boreal Forest is the largest boreal forest ecosystem in North America that is free of roads. It covers an area about the size of France. The plant life in this forest can store the equivalent of 27 years of worldwide **carbon emissions**.

ARCTIC OCEAN

Scandinavian Taiga,
Scandinavia

Urals Montane Taiga,
Russia

Eastern Siberian Taiga,
Russia

ASIA

EUROPE

**Trans-Baikal
Coniferous Forest,**
Mongolia

Sakhalin Island Taiga,
Russia

PACIFIC
OCEAN

AFRICA

Russian Boreal Forest

Location: Russia
Size: 2.9 million square miles (7.5 million sq. km)
Fact: The Russian Boreal Forest makes up the largest
forested region in the world. This forest contains few tree
species, mostly birch, pine, spruce, and fir. The area is home
to more than 55 percent of the coniferous trees on Earth.

SOUTH
ATLANTIC
OCEAN

INDIAN
OCEAN

AUSTRALIA

Caledonian Forest

Location: Scotland
Size: 58 square miles (150 sq. km)
Fact: The Caledonian Forest of Scotland
once covered 5,792 square miles (15,000
sq. km) across the Scottish Highlands.
Today, only 35 small tracks of the original
forest remain. Some of the remaining trees
in this forest are more than 300 years old.

ANTARCTICA

Boreal Forest Climate

Boreal forest rivers provide drinking water and food for land mammals and habitat for fish and aquatic birds.

The boreal forest lies below the arctic tundra. Cold temperatures can last from October to May. The average temperature for six to eight months of the year is about 14° F (−10° C). Annual snowfall varies, ranging from 12 to 39 inches (30 to 100 cm). Cold winter temperatures and winds prevent snow from melting between storms. In the boreal forest, summers are usually short, cool, and moist. Temperatures average between 59° and 77° F (15° and 25° C). Some summer days can be hot and humid with temperatures rising above 86° F (30° C).

Precipitation

Precipitation falls as rain in summer and snow in winter. Cool temperatures slow **evaporation**. Many boreal forests have thick layers of moss that act as sponges to soak up water and keep the ground moist. Much of the rain and melted snow is trapped in wetlands. In some places, the ground is permanently frozen.

Sunlight

The slant of the Sun's rays during each season has a major effect on the amount of daylight that boreal forests receive. During winter, the nights are long and dark. There may be no sunlight for many days. In contrast, a summer day can have as many as 20 hours of daylight.

Permafrost

In some parts of the boreal forest, long periods of freezing weather cause permafrost. In these areas, the ground remains frozen for much of the year. However, the active layer, or top layer, may thaw, allowing plant roots to absorb water and grow. It is difficult for plants to grow long roots in such shallow soil. Their growth may be stunted, or they may fall over easily.

Microclimates

Within the harsh climate of the boreal forests, there are many microclimates. These are small areas that are warmer or colder, wetter or drier, more or less shaded, or less windy than normal. Overhanging evergreen branches reduce the cold wind and provide pockets of warm shelter. In many places, the forest floor is covered with fallen pine needles, twigs, and leaves that slowly decompose, creating new **habitats** for many insects and spiders. Loose bark and crevices on trees and fallen logs also provide shelter for insects, birds, and small mammals. Snow insulates many small mammals and insects throughout the harsh winter. Beneath deep snowdrifts, voles, mice, shrews, and a variety of insects and spiders live in warm tunnels and burrows. Some small plants can grow under the snow during winter.

Eco Facts

In eastern Siberia, the average January temperature dips to −58° F (−50° C). At this temperature, exhaled breath freezes into ice crystals.

The coldest air temperatures in North America occur in the taiga. In January 1971, a record low temperature of −79.8° F (−62° C) was recorded in Prospect Creek, Alaska.

Autumn is the shortest season in boreal forest ecosystems. ▮

Boreal Forest Seasons

Coniferous trees have adapted to survive snowy boreal forest winters. Their cone shape allows snow to fall when it becomes too heavy for the branches.

The Woodland, or Northern, Cree have lived in the boreal forest for centuries. The Woodland Cree have identified six seasons in the boreal forest. These are *sikwan* (spring), *mithoskamin* (break-up), *nipin* (summer), *takwakin* (autumn), *mikiskaw* (freeze-up), and *pipon* (winter).

Freeze-up and Break-up

Mikiskaw, the time of freeze-up, occurs between autumn and winter, usually in October. This is a time when the trees lose their leaves or needles and lakes are covered with ice.

Mithoskamin, the season of break-up, occurs from late March to late May or early June. During this time, snow melts, showing patches of bare ground. This season lasts until the thick lake ice melts. It can take a long time for lake ice to melt because it can be 3 feet (1 meter) thick. During *mithoskamin,* there are long hours of daylight, but little moisture is released from frozen ground and lakes. Warm winds, along with up to 20 hours of sunshine each day, dry out the trees. Fires often occur during this time.

Forest Fires

In most years, thousands of fires break out across boreal forests. Lightning strikes cause one-third of these forest fires. The remaining two-thirds of forest fires are started by careless people. The average lightning fire is almost 10 times larger than fires caused by people. Each part of the forest will burn at least once every 150 years.

Eco Facts

One year after a fire in Alaska, 2,000 spruce, 500 poplar, and 800 birch seedlings per acre (0.40 hectare) were counted.

Jack pines depend on forest fires to distribute most of their seeds. Their pine cones are sealed with a resin that only opens in intense heat. Jack pine seeds can withstand temperatures of 1,300° F (700° C).

The forest provides a large amount of fuel for fires. Conifer needles and branches are highly flammable, especially during dry weather. Lichens burn easily and grow on many tree branches.

New Growth

New growth begins almost immediately after a fire. Plants sprout through the ash-covered soil. The wind blows plant seeds to the burned area. Other plants, such as fireweed, thistle, willow, birch, and aspen, lie dormant in the soil. Some tree species have roots living underground. Birch trees grow new sprouts around the burned rim of trunks. Heat from fires opens jack pine cones, spilling seeds on the forest floor. As the forest grows, trees become taller, blocking out sunlight. Trees that enjoy shade, such as the spruce and balsam fir, may become the most common species in the boreal forest.

| The smoke from forest fires can travel great distances, even to other continents. |

Life in Boreal Forests

Boreal forest ecosystems are home to many forms of life. As winter approaches, many species of birds, butterflies, salmon, and mammals migrate to warmer climates. In spring, these animals return to boreal forests to enjoy the abundant food the lush forest vegetation provides. Some hardy bird species remain in the boreal forest throughout the year.

Producers

Trees and other plants found in boreal forests act as producers for other organisms in the ecosystem. Producers absorb energy from the Sun and convert it into usable forms of energy such as sugar. They make this energy through a process called **photosynthesis**. Producers found in boreal forests include all types of pine, fir, and spruce trees, as well as moss, lichen, shrubs, and other plants.

Primary Consumers

The animals that rely on producers as a food source are called primary consumers. When a primary consumer feeds on a producer, the energy made by the producer is transferred to the primary consumer. Examples of primary consumers found in boreal forests include some insects and birds, as well as mammals such as hares, beavers, caribou, and moose.

Boreal Forest Food Pyramid

The transfer of energy in an ecosystem begins with producers and moves up the energy pyramid to the tertiary consumers. Organisms at each level of the pyramid receive energy from the organisms in the level below them.

Outside of the pyramid are the decomposers. They break down the dead and decaying organic matter left behind when plants and animals die. For this reason, decomposers receive energy from organisms in all levels of the energy pyramid.

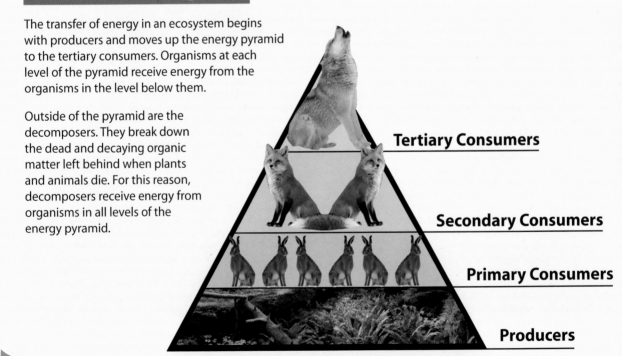

Tertiary Consumers

Secondary Consumers

Primary Consumers

Producers

Boreal Forest Food Web

Another way to study the flow of energy through an ecosystem is by examining food chains and food webs. A food chain shows how a producer feeds a primary consumer, which then feeds a secondary consumer, and so on. However, most organisms feed on many different food sources. This practice causes food chains to interconnect, creating a food web.

In this example, the **red line** represents one food chain from the blueberries, willow ptarmigan, and grizzly bear. The **blue line** from the pine tree, beaver, and coyote form another food chain. These food chains connect in several places. The grizzly bear also eats beavers, and the coyote also eats willow ptarmigans. This series of connections forms a complex food web.

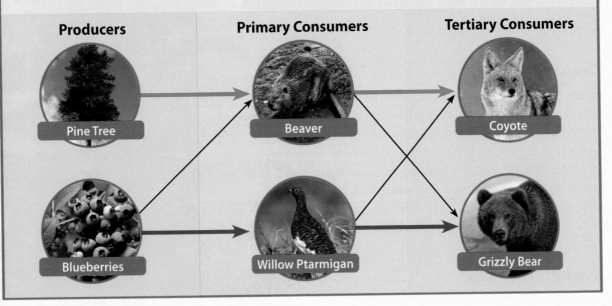

Secondary and Tertiary Consumers

Secondary consumers feed on both producers and primary consumers. In boreal forests, secondary consumers include large insects, many birds, and mammals, including mice, squirrels, and martens. Larger carnivores, such as bears and wolves, and some birds of prey, such as hawks and eagles, are called tertiary consumers. Tertiary consumers feed on secondary consumers.

Decomposers

Fungi, such as mushrooms, and many types of bacteria live in boreal forest ecosystems. These organisms are called decomposers because they eat dead and decaying **organic** materials. Decomposers speed up the process of breaking down dead organic materials and releasing their **nutrients** into the soil. These nutrients are then absorbed by the roots of trees and other plants.

Plants

The bark of an aspen tree is edible.

Deciduous Trees

Some boreal forest trees are deciduous. These trees lose their leaves in autumn and regrow them in the spring. This allows the trees to use less energy during winter months. Fewer branches break from the buildup of snow and ice as well. Most of these deciduous trees are broadleaf, such as birch, aspen, and poplar, or shrubs, such as willow, alder, and blueberry.

Coniferous Trees

Most boreal-forest trees are coniferous evergreens. Conifers keep their green leaves for more than one season, allowing the tree to begin photosynthesis early in spring. Conifers have needle-shaped leaves with a waxy coating. These leaves lose less water in spring and summer than broad leaves. Most evergreens lose their needles after two or three years. Some, such as spruce, keep their leaves for as long as eight or nine years. Conifers, such as larch and tamarack, lose their leaves every year.

Spruce trees are common in North America.

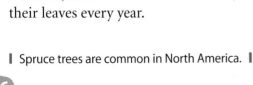

Eco Facts

Many small, carnivorous plants, such as pitcher plants, sundews, and bladderworts, live in boreal forest ecosystems. These plants lure insects using color, odor, and nectar. They trap insects using suction cups, sticky flypaper, or pitfall traps.

Taiga trees harden during autumn. Hardening enables them to withstand temperatures as cold as –40° F (–40° C).

Aspen trees that share the same root system are considered one organism. They can stretch more than 100 acres (40 ha) and have thousands of tree trunks.

Fungi

Many types of fungi grow in boreal forests. Fungi often grow near other plants. Mushrooms are fungi that come in a variety of shapes, sizes, and colors. They grow in soil and on living and dead plants, such as trees. Other types of fungi grow on the roots of conifer trees. These fungi look like thin hairs. They help tree roots absorb moisture and minerals to make food.

The moist ground of boreal forests provides an ideal habitat for many types of mushrooms.

Lichens

Lichens form when algae and fungus grow together. Lichens come in a variety of shapes and sizes. They live on the ground, as well as on logs, rocks, and tree branches. Some lichens are important food sources for caribou and reindeer. These lichens are called reindeer mosses.

There are about 25,000 species of lichen.

Moss

Moss is a small, feathery plant that grows on the forest floor and in bogs. In cool, moist places with acidic soil, moss can grow from 3 to 7 feet (1 to 2 m) thick. Moss can absorb huge amounts of moisture. Sphagnum moss can hold up to 20 times its weight in water.

Mosses cover about one-third of the ground in boreal forest ecosystems.

Birds

Migrant Birds

During the winter, the boreal forest bird population drops from about 320 species to about 30 species of birds. In the most northern regions, only two or three species remain. Most migrant birds fall into two groups. The first group travels short distances. In North America, these birds migrate to the southern United States. Birds in this group include bald and golden eagles, great blue herons, loons, kingfishers, tree swallows, warblers, sparrows, and hawks. The second group of birds travels longer distances to tropical climates, such as Mexico and Central and South America. This group includes ospreys, peregrine falcons, cuckoos, martins, redstarts, tanagers, sparrows, swallows, and warblers. In Europe and Asia, long-distance migratory birds travel to Africa or other tropical destinations.

An osprey's wingspan is about 5 to 6 feet (1.5 to 1.8 m).

Non-migrant Birds

Some bird species remain in boreal forest ecosystems all year. North American birds in this group include goshawks, grouse, ravens, nuthatches, kinglets, jays, woodpeckers, chickadees, crossbills, and grosbeaks. Many owls, including the great horned, great gray, boreal, barred, and hawk, are year-round residents, too.

The great horned owl is named for the tufts of feathers on its head, which look like horns.

Eco Facts

To save energy during long, cold nights, some birds lower their internal body temperature. Chickadees can lower their body temperature at night from 104° F (40° C) to 86° F (30° C).

Gray jays nest from late February to early March, when temperatures are as cold as −20° F (−29° C). They lay eggs before April.

Scatter Hoarding

Many year-round bird species store food for winter. Gray jays begin hoarding in June. They store hundreds of food items, including insects, spiders, berries, and mushrooms. Jays pack the food into pellets and coat them with saliva. Then, they cram the pellets into cracks in the bark of a tree or in a cluster of conifer needles. Chickadees are also hoarders. These birds store seeds, berries, and insects. Each bird hides thousands of food items each day in needle clusters, lichens, bark, curled leaves, and broken branches. Some chickadees use silk from spider webs and cocoons to hold the seeds in place.

Black-capped chickadees communicate using at least 15 different calls.

Burrowing

Many small birds, including chickadees, redpolls, sparrows, and snow buntings, burrow under the snow. Using their feet, wings, and beak, some small birds can dig a tunnel under the snow up to 8 inches (20 cm) deep. Grouse and ptarmigan also burrow under the snow. To shelter from wind and cold, boreal-forest birds often roost in thick conifer branches or squeeze into tight tree cavities.

The white-tailed ptarmigan is the smallest of all ptarmigans.

Mammals

Herbivores and Carnivores

In boreal forest ecosystems, mammals range from the shrew to the grizzly bear. **Herbivores** include moose, deer, muskrats, and voles. **Carnivores** use a variety of hunting strategies to catch their prey. Wolverines hunt alone, while wolves stalk their prey in groups. Many of the same mammals are found in boreal forests around the world.

The lynx often watches its prey from above before pouncing to catch its meal.

Dwellings

Most mammals live in protected microclimates. They build dens, dig burrows, or create tents under conifer branches. Crevices and holes in trees and logs also provide shelter. Deep snow provides **insulation**. In these shelters, the temperature reaches 25° F (−4° C) when the weather is −40° F (−40° C) outdoors. Some mammals, such as mice and voles, huddle together in burrows during the winter. Other mammals build year-round dwellings. Beavers build dams made of logs, branches, and rocks that they seal with mud from lakes and ponds. Much of the dam is underwater. Beavers cut vast supplies of wood to feed on during the winter and store fat in their tails during the summer and autumn.

Beavers build curved dams in rivers that have fast-moving water.

Eco Facts

Unlike other species of squirrels, tree squirrels have no cheek pouches.

Bears usually eat between 5,000 and 8,000 calories each day. Humans only eat between 2,000 and 3,000 calories each day. In late summer and autumn, bears eat two to three times more food than normal. During this time, they gain about 1.5 to 2.2 pounds (0.7 to 1 kilograms) every day.

Wolverines are also called skunk bears, devil bears, and gluttons. A large male weighs about 60 pounds (27 kg). Wolverines can tackle prey as large as moose and caribou.

Camouflage

Some boreal forest animals change the color and texture of their fur coats depending on the season. Snowshoe hares turn white in winter and brown in summer. This helps them blend in with the snow or soil. Their winter coats contain clear, white hairs that have air pockets inside. These air pockets act as extra insulation against the cold. Hares also have large, furry feet that act as snowshoes, allowing the animals to run over the surface of the snow without sinking.

It takes about 10 weeks for a snowshoe hare's fur to change color.

Hibernation

Some mammals gain large amounts of weight in autumn. These animals **hibernate** throughout the winter. Both black and grizzly bears enter their dens in late autumn and do not leave until spring. During this time, bears maintain a state of deep sleep. Their heart rate slows, and their body temperature drops.

A grizzly bear can spend up to eight months in its den before coming out again.

Boreal Forests in Danger

Animals in danger of becoming extinct are classified as endangered. This means there are so few of the species alive that they need protection to survive. The grizzly bear, Siberian tiger, pine marten, whooping crane, and peregrine falcon are just a few of the boreal forest's animals that are considered to be endangered. In the United States, it is illegal to hunt or harm endangered animals.

Pollution traps large amounts of **greenhouse gases** in Earth's atmosphere. The global climate is currently warming 10 times faster than at the end of the last ice age. Many scientists believe this warming trend will continue, permanently changing the boreal forest. Snow may melt earlier in the season, summers may become drier, forest fires may occur more frequently, and permafrost may melt. The southern part of the boreal forest may disappear completely, becoming parkland and arid grassland. It will be difficult for plant and animal species to adjust and survive.

Clear-cutting, a logging technique in which all of the trees in an area are removed at once, destroys habitat and disrupts normal forest growth. Plant and animal species lose their natural habitats. Overharvesting of animals through commercial

Timeline of Human Activity in Boreal Forests

Glaciers gradually retreat, allowing European and North American boreal forest plant and animal species to begin migrating north.

The world's oldest newspaper still in publication is founded in Stockholm, Sweden. The paper is produced using pulp from Europe's boreal forests.

Logging activity by European settlers in North America reaches the southern edge of the boreal forest.

16,000 BC — **7,000 BC** — **1645 AD** — **1670** — **1880s** — **1908**

White spruce trees in what is now Western Canada migrate northward rapidly, covering about 1,240 miles (2,000 km) in just 1,000 years.

The Hudson's Bay Company is founded to trade goods for animal furs in the boreal forests of North America.

A small asteroid explodes over Siberia, Russia, resulting in the destruction of about 800 square miles (2,072 sq. km) of boreal forest.

hunting and fishing can cause problems for certain species. Recreational vehicles and the roads built for them disrupt habitats, breeding and nesting areas, and migrating pathways.

Hydroelectric dams built on major rivers change the water flow, flooding thousands of acres (hectares) of land. This destroys habitats and migration routes for salmon and caribou. Large numbers of wildlife drown or become displaced.

Boreal forests are experiencing deforestation as rapidly as rain forests.

The loss of its natural habitat brings the whooping crane to near extinction. The creation of the Wood Buffalo National Park in Canada in 1922 and the Aransas National Wildlife Refuge in Texas in 1937 provide some of the only natural habitats for whooping cranes in North America.

Roughly half of the world's boreal forests, or 3.5 million square miles (9.25 million sq. km), remain undisturbed by human activity. Most of this undisturbed area is in Canada and Russia.

The government of Alaska and the U.S. Forest Service agree to the Tongass Land Management Plan. The plan sets aside certain areas for logging while protecting other key areas of the Tongass National Forest.

1922　　**1980s**　　**2000**　　**2003**　　**2008**　　**2010**

Woodland caribou only inhabit 51 percent of their original rangeland in the North American boreal forest.

A severe heat wave hits Europe, causing extremely dry conditions in Russia's boreal forests. Forest fires during this period destroy about 85,000 square miles (220,000 sq. km) of boreal forest ecosystems.

About 1,500 scientists from around the world call for the protection of boreal forest ecosystems in North America. Only 10 percent of North America's boreal forests are protected under law.

Science in Boreal Forests

Electronically tagging an animal allows scientists to monitor its movement throughout the animal's entire life.

One hundred years ago, few people ventured into the vast boreal forest. However, the Woodland Cree adapted to the harsh living conditions. They made snowshoes and sleighs to travel across the land. They also built snow houses called quin-zhee. To make a quin-zhee, the Cree shoveled snow into a pile and let it harden for at least one hour. Then, they burrowed into the snow, making a hollow, cave-like space. Inside the quin-zhee, body heat and insulating snow warmed the temperature to 28° F (–2° C). This was warmer than the outdoor temperature.

Technology Uses

Today, new technologies help scientists navigate the boreal forest and learn about its plants, animals, and ecosystems. Scientists often study samples from forest areas to learn about different organisms and how many species live there. They use live traps and nets to collect birds and animals. Scientists record the age, gender, condition, and weight of each animal. They also mark animals with identification tags or bands. Scientists use the data they collect to understand how ecosystems change over time.

Tracking Animals

Scientists also use radio telemetry, radio tagging, or radio tracking. A transmitter attached to an animal sends a signal to a receiver. Scientists use the radio signal to track the animal's movements. This method of tracking provides a great deal of information about an animal's habitat, territory, migration, activity, and life history.

Eco Facts

If the sky is cloudy, forest fires might not be detected with remote sensing monitors.

Scientists have used GPS devices to study the movements and feeding habits of many animals, including deer.

Satellite Imaging

Remote satellite sensing uses satellite images to show what types of trees grow in an area, where wetlands and lakes occur, where fires are burning, the effects of climate change, and areas affected by human development. Remote satellite sensing helps scientists maintain healthy forests. Scientists can also use remote satellite sensing to monitor, map, and model forest fires. **Infrared** satellite images show burning vegetation. They show the location of active forest fires, how the fire is behaving or moving, and the size of the area burned.

Global Positioning System

The Global Positioning System (GPS) uses satellite technology to find exact locations any place on Earth. People use GPS to navigate the boreal forest.

The satellite system for GPS gives every square foot (0.1 square meter) on Earth a unique address.

Working in Boreal Forests

Researchers in boreal forest ecosystems work in one of the most challenging environments on Earth.

From working with animals or plants in the boreal forest to researching the effect of climate change in boreal forest ecosystems, most forest-related jobs require a background in biology, ecology, or environmental studies. Choosing a career in wildlife conservation, biology, or forest management is ideal for people interested in ecosystems and animals.

Wildlife Biologist

Duties

Studies wildlife and their environments

Education

Bachelor's, master's, or doctoral degree in biology, zoology, environmental studies, or ecology

Interests

Biology, the environment, conservation, science, animals, plants, ecosystems

Wildlife biologists enjoy learning about animals and how different species relate to each other and their environments. They study wildlife, prepare environmental projects, perform field research, analyze data, inventory plant and animal communities, and practice environmental impact studies. Wildlife biologists also prepare information in brochures, books, and slide shows for presentations to schools and other groups.

Other Boreal Forest Jobs

Ecologist

Studies the relationship between living things and their environments

Forester

Works to ensure people use forests wisely and limit harm to forest habitat and wildlife

Environmental Consultant

Studies the ways in which pollution and human activity affect boreal forest ecosystems

Alan Rabinowitz

Alan Robert Rabinowitz (1953–) is an American wildlife biologist, zoologist, and conservationist. He earned the nickname "the Indiana Jones of wildlife science" for his many journeys into the most dangerous places on Earth. Rabinowitz has made it his mission to protect the world's 36 species of large cats.

In 1974, Rabinowitz received his bachelor's degree in biology and chemistry. By 1981, he had earned a doctoral degree in wildlife ecology from the University of Tennessee.

Over the next 30 years, Rabinowitz worked with the Wildlife Conservation Society. He worked mostly in Asia during this time and quickly advanced within the society. From 2006 to 2008, Rabinowitz served as the executive director of the society's science and exploration program.

In 2008, Rabinowitz became the president of Panthera. Panthera is an international non-profit foundation dedicated to saving large cats, such as tigers, lions, jaguars, and leopards.

Rabinowitz has written six books and more than 100 articles for scientific journals. He has also received many awards for his work.

Make a Cast of Animal Tracks

B oreal forest animals leave their footprints or tracks in the snow and on the wet ground. You can learn how to identify the tracks of different animals and then try to make your own in plaster.

Materials

disposable plastic container

paper plate

animal tracks in sand or mud

plaster of Paris

1 Mix a batch of plaster of Paris. Be sure to follow the directions on the package.

2 Pour the plaster into the plastic container.

3 Explore your community to find interesting animal tracks. If you find some, fill them with plaster. Once the plaster hardens, you can lift it from the tracks. Can you tell what sort of animal made the tracks? Are they from a cat or dog? Could they be from another animal, such as a deer?

4 Pour some plaster onto a paper plate. Make sure the plaster is about 1 inch (2.5 cm) thick.

5 If you have a pet dog or cat, gently press the animal's paw into the plaster. If you do not have a dog or cat, press your bare foot into the plaster. Wait for the plaster to harden. How is this track similar to the tracks you found outside? How is it different?

Create a Food Web

Use this book, and research on the Internet, to create a food web of boreal forest ecosystem plants and animals. Start by finding at least three organisms of each type—producers, primary consumers, secondary consumers, and tertiary consumers. Then, begin linking these organisms together into food chains. Draw the arrows of each food chain in a different color. Use a **red** pen or crayon for one food chain and **green** and **blue** for the others. You should find that many of these food chains connect, creating a food web. Add the rest of the arrows to complete the food web using a pencil or **black** pen.

Once your food web is complete, use it to answer the following questions.

1 How would removing one organism from your food web affect the other organisms in the web?

2 What would happen to the rest of the food web if the producers were taken away?

3 How would decomposers fit into the food web?

Sample Food Web

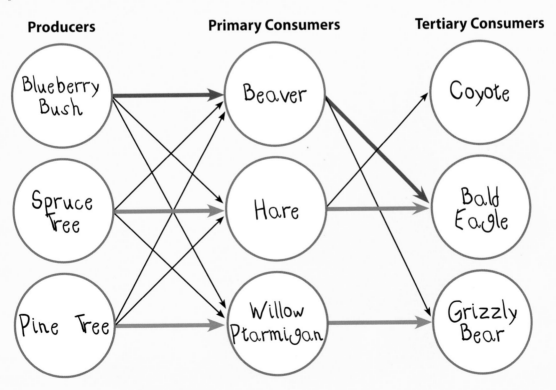

Producers   **Primary Consumers**   **Tertiary Consumers**

Blueberry Bush   Beaver   Coyote

Spruce Tree   Hare   Bald Eagle

Pine Tree   Willow Ptarmigan   Grizzly Bear

Eco Challenge

1. The boreal forest appears on how many continents? Name them.

2. How many seasons do the Woodland Cree recognize in the boreal forest?

3. How many months have temperatures below freezing in the boreal forest?

4. Which country contains the largest boreal forest area?

5. What are three other names for boreal forest?

6. How are most forest fires started?

7. What do most boreal forest birds do in winter?

8. Name four endangered boreal forest animals.

9. What are the most common trees in the boreal forest?

10. What attracts so many birds to the boreal forest each spring?

Answers

1. Three; North America, Europe, and Asia
2. Six
3. Six to eight months
4. Russia
5. Coniferous forest, northern forest, and taiga
6. Lightning and human carelessness
7. Migrate
8. Grizzly bear, Siberian tiger, whooping crane, and peregrine falcon
9. Coniferous trees
10. Wetlands and swarms of insects

Glossary

camouflages: uses protective coloring to blend into natural surroundings

carbon emissions: carbon dioxide gas released into the air when fuels such as oil and coal are burned

carnivores: animals that hunt other animals for food

coniferous: trees that have cones and needles

deciduous: trees that lose their leaves at the end of the growing season

ecosystem: a community of living things sharing an environment

evaporation: the process of changing from liquid to a gas

greenhouse gases: atmospheric gases that reflect heat back to Earth

habitats: the natural homes of plants or animals

herbivores: plant-eating animals

hibernate: spend winter resting or sleeping to save energy

infrared: invisible wavelengths

insulation: something that keeps heat in

isotherm: a line drawn on a map linking areas of the same climate

lichens: organisms made up of algae and fungi that grow on tree trunks, rocks, and the ground

migratory: move from one area to another

nutrients: substances that feed plants or animals

organic: materials that come from living things

organisms: living things

photosynthesis: the process in which a green plant uses sunlight to change water and carbon dioxide into food for itself

species: a group of similar plants and animals that can mate together

Index

Log on to www.av2books.com

AV[2] by Weigl brings you media enhanced books that support active learning. Go to www.av2books.com, and enter the special code found on page 2 of this book. You will gain access to enriched and enhanced content that supplements and complements this book. Content includes video, audio, web links, quizzes, a slide show, and activities.

Audio
Listen to sections of the book read aloud.

Video
Watch informative video clips.

Embedded Weblinks
Gain additional information for research.

Try This!
Complete activities and hands-on experiments.

WHAT'S ONLINE?

Try This!	**Embedded Weblinks**	**Video**	**EXTRA FEATURES**
Map boreal forests around the world.	Learn more about boreal forests.	Watch a video about boreal forests.	**Audio** Listen to sections of the book read aloud.
Find out more about animals that live in boreal forests.	Find current weather forecasts in a boreal forest.	Watch a video about an animal that lives in a boreal forest.	**Key Words** Study vocabulary, and complete a matching word activity.
Test your knowledge of human activity in boreal forests.	Learn how to identify different plants in boreal forests.		
Write a descriptive paragraph about a day in the life of a scientist working in a boreal forest.	Read about current research in boreal forests.		**Slide Show** View images and captio and prepare a presentat
	Learn more about food chains.		**Quizzes** Test your knowledge.

AV[2] was built to bridge the gap between print and digital. We encourage you to tell us what you like and what you want to see in the future.

Sign up to be an AV[2] Ambassador at www.av2books.com/ambassador.